If you were me and lived in...
PORTUGAL

A Child's Introduction to Cultures Around the World

Carole P. Roman

To my Aunt Junie and Uncle Art who loved to travel and always brought back a piece of the country they visited.

ISBN-10: 1495379930

ISBN-13: 978-1495379932

Disclaimer:
Please note that there may be differences in dialect that will vary according to region. Multiple individuals (from each country) were used as sources for the pronunciation key but you should be aware of the possibility of alternative pronunciations.

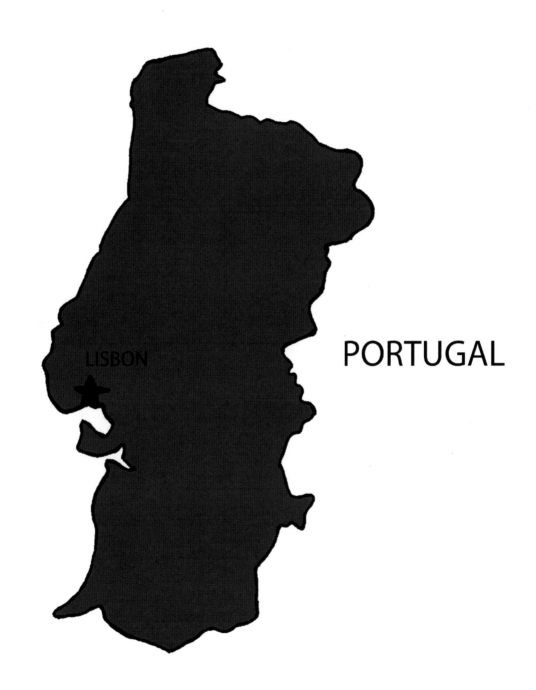

LISBON

PORTUGAL

If you were me and lived in Portugal (Por- tu- gal), you would find yourself on the Iberian (I-beer-ee-an) Peninsula in the most western country on the mainland of Europe. Spain is on its eastern border and the Atlantic Ocean is on the west. It was named for the second largest city, Porto, whose Latin name was Portus Cale (Port-tu Call).

You might live with your family in the capital city, Lisbon (Liz-bun). Not only is it one of the oldest cities in the world, it is the oldest in Western Europe. Six hundred years ago, in search of new trade routes for spices and other riches, the Portuguese (Por-tu-geeze) sailed out and colonized many different parts of the world, so that today 240 million people speak the Portuguese language.

4

If you are a boy and born in Portugal, your parents might have named you Tomás (Toe-mas), Afonso (A-fon-zho), or Martins (Mar-teens). They could have named your sister Maria (Ma-ree-ya), Joana (Wa-nah), or Leonor (Lee-on-or).

6

When you need your mommy, you might shout, "Olá, Máe " (O-la May), which means, "Hey, Mom." When Daddy tucks you in at night, you always say, "Amo-te paizinho" (A-mo-te pa-iz-nho). Can you guess what you are saying to your pai (pay)?

When shopping with avó (a-vo), she might buy you a rooster of Barcelos (Bar-chel-los). It is a beloved and colorful symbol of Portugal. She would use euros (ur-roos) to purchase it.

Can you guess who avó is?

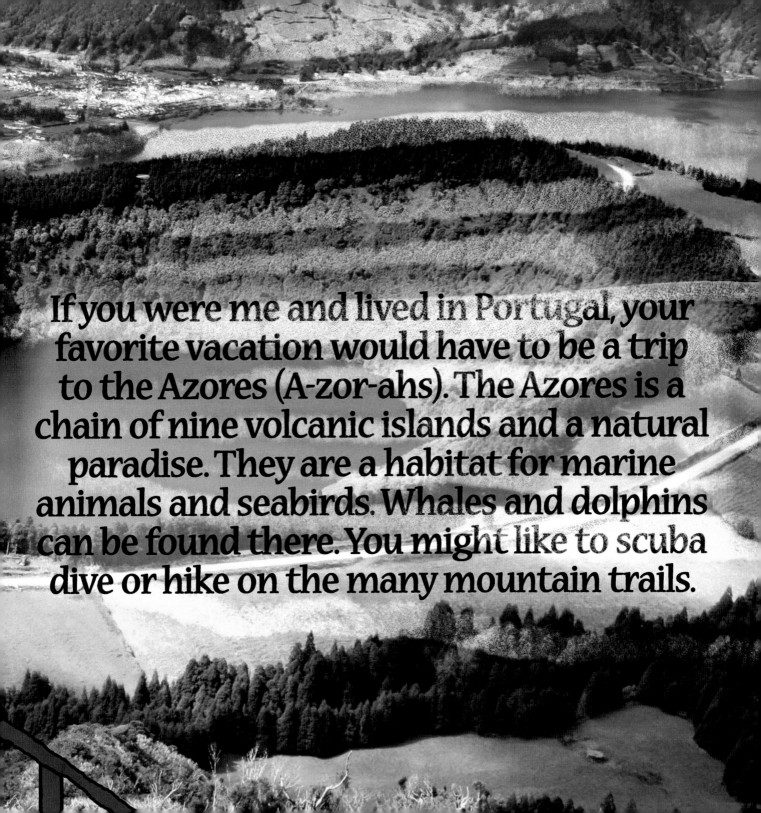

If you were me and lived in Portugal, your favorite vacation would have to be a trip to the Azores (A-zor-ahs). The Azores is a chain of nine volcanic islands and a natural paradise. They are a habitat for marine animals and seabirds. Whales and dolphins can be found there. You might like to scuba dive or hike on the many mountain trails.

You might like to eat bacalhau (bak-al-hau) or salted cod if you lived in Portugal. It is a popular food and it is said there are 365 ways to prepare it, one for each day of the year. Grilled sardines would be another favorite fish. Arroz de marisco (Ar-ros dee mar-iz-co) is rice with lots of seafood and also greatly enjoyed. Why do you think there is so much fish on the menu?

For dessert, your mom would make you pastélis de nata (pas-tel-is dee na-ta), which is a custard tart sprinkled with cinnamon.

14

Of course, futebol (fute-bol) or soccer would be your favorite game. You would like to remind people that some say ping pong was invented in Portugal.

Maybe your baby sister would play with a boneca (bon-ec-a) while you watch television.

16

in February and would be your favorite time of the year. It is a huge celebration before Lent when many people give up meat before Easter. Carnevale literally means "put away the meat." Streets are filled with parties and colorful

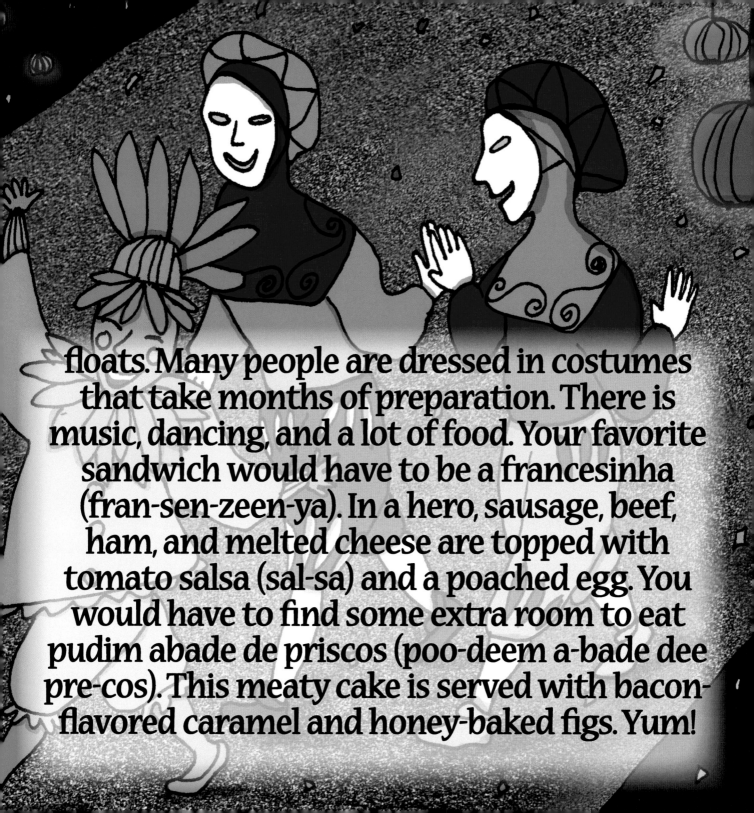

floats. Many people are dressed in costumes that take months of preparation. There is music, dancing, and a lot of food. Your favorite sandwich would have to be a francesinha (fran-sen-zeen-ya). In a hero, sausage, beef, ham, and melted cheese are topped with tomato salsa (sal-sa) and a poached egg. You would have to find some extra room to eat pudim abade de priscos (poo-deem a-bade dee pre-cos). This meaty cake is served with bacon-flavored caramel and honey-baked figs. Yum!

Eu gosto de escola (Oo gos-too dee es-co-la) is what you would tell everybody when they ask if you like school.

So you see, if you were me, how life in Portugal could really be.

22

Pronunciation Guide

"Amo-te paizinho" (A-mo-te pa-iz-nho)- "I love you, Daddy."

Afonso (A-fon-zho)- popular boy's name.

arroz de mariso (ar-ros dee-mar-iz-co)- rice with seafood.

Avó (A-vo)- Grandmother.

Azores (Ah-zor-ahs)- nine volcanic islands where people vacation and see animals in their natural habitat.

bacalhau (bak-al-hau)- salted cod.

Barcelos (Bar-chel-los)- a town where the colorful carved roosters are made.

boneca (bon-ec-a)- doll.

Carnevale (Ca-ne-val)- a big holiday in February where there is lots of parades, dancing, and food.

Eu gosto de escola (Oo gos-too dee es-co-la)- I like school.

euros (ur-oos)- currency.

francesinha (fran-sen-zeen-ya)- huge sandwich filled with lots of meat and topped with an egg.

futbole (fut-bol)- ball game also known as soccer.

Iberian (I-beer-ee-an)- name of the peninsula where both Portugal and Spain are located.

Joana (Wa-nah)- popular girl's name.

Leonor (Lee-on-or)- popular girl's name.

Lisbon (Liz-bun)- capital of Portugal.

Maria (Ma-ree-ya)- popular girl's name.

Martins (Mar- teens)- popular boy's name.

"Olá, Máe." (O-la May)- "Hey, Mom."

Pai (Pay)- Dad.

pastélis de nata (pas-tel-is dee na-ta)- custard tart sprinkled with cinnamon.

Portugal (Por-tu-gal)- a country on the western end of Europe.

Portuguese (Por-tu-geeze)- language spoken in Portugal.

Portus Cale (Port-tu Call)- original name of Portugal.

pudim abade de priscos (poo-deem a-bade dee pre-cos)- meaty cake served with bacon flavored caramel and honey baked figs.

Tomás (Toe-mas)- popular boy's name.

Made in the USA
Columbia, SC
19 December 2019